Cool HIGH-TECH Jobs

by Richard Spilsbury

raintree

a Capstone company — publishers for children

Engage Literacy is published in the UK by Raintree.
Raintree is an imprint of Capstone Global Library Limited, a company incorporated in England and Wales having its registered office at 264 Banbury Road, Oxford, OX2 7DY – Registered company number: 6695582

www.raintree.co.uk

© 2018 by Raintree. All rights reserved. No part of this publication may be reproduced, stored in a retrieval system, or transmitted in any way or by any means, electronic, mechanical, photocopying, recording or otherwise, without the prior written permission of Capstone Global Library Limited.

Editorial credits
Carrie Braulick Sheely, editor; Richard Parker, designer; Steve Walker, production specialist

Image credits
Alamy: dpa picture alliance archive, 23, Ryan McGinnis, 51; Glow Images: Cultura RF/Monty Rakusen, 41; NASA, 57 (bottom), Bill Ingalls, 57 (top); Newscom: DanitaDelimont.com/David R. Frazier, 43, EPA/DIEGO AZUBEL, 31, Richard B. Levine, 60, Sipa USA/Kris Tripplaar, 5, VWPics/Ton Koene, 62 (bottom), ZUMA Press/Jim Damaske, 37, ZUMA Press/Media Drum World/G. Brad Lewis, 47, ZUMA Press/Smityuk Yuri, 35; Rebecca Coats, 48 (both); Science Source: James King-Holmes, 39; Shutterstock: Alexey Y. Petrov, 55, ARKHIPOV ALEKSEY, 13, ChameleonsEye, 52, Elena Pavlovich, cover (bottom), goodluz, 59, HABRDA, 42, higyou, 8, Jeff Whyte, 9, Leonel Calara, 21, Monkey Business Images, back cover, 33 (bottom), Ociacia, 62 (top), Patrizio Martorana, 45 (bottom), Peter Aleksandrov, 29, Peter Sobolev, cover (right), Pressmaster, 45 (top), ProStockStudio, 15, Rawpixel.com, 18, Rommel Canlas, 24, seregalsv, 11, supergenijalac, 7, Supphachal Salaeman, throughout (background), Tinxi, 33 (top), Tinxi, 61, Tonhom1009, 62 (middle), vitstudio, 40, WAYHOME studio, cover (top left), Willyam Bradberry, cover (left), ymgerman, 27, Your Design, 17; U.S. Air Force, 10

Bibliography
p. 21: Newzoo. 2016 Global Games Market Report. June 2016. http://resources.newzoo.com/hubfs/Reports/Newzoo_Free_2016_Global_Games_Market_Report.pdf?hsCtaTracking=df924a51-0302-4d95-b440-56273fbce61b%7C4b95d366-0ad4-4d6d-b0b5-54e34fd454fb&__hstc=133451409.f98abb45bb6460b3d1b6b4a6df6ddb83.1487878542255.1487878542255.1488985959280.2&__hssc=133451409.16.1488985959280&__hsfp=3603054584

pp. 48–49: Rebecca Coats. Personal Interview. 25 October 2016.

21 20 19 18 17
10 9 8 7 6 5 4 3 2 1
Printed and bound in China.

Cool High-Tech Jobs

ISBN: 978 1 4747 4590 1

Contents

World of high-tech jobs 4

Robotics 6

Computers 14

Gaming 20

Product design 26

Biomedicine 34

Earth science .46

Transport and energy 52

Glossary 63

Index 64

Introduction

World of high-tech jobs

Some of the coolest jobs on the planet use Science, *Technology*, *Engineering* and Maths (STEM) skills. Would you like to invent robots, design smartphones or build space rockets? These awesome jobs and many more involve STEM skills, and they could be in your future!

The world of STEM

Let's take a closer look at STEM.

• Science is about understanding the world around us, such as exploring space or ways to power machines.

• Technology uses science to solve problems and invent useful things, such as laptops and lasers.

• Engineering involves designing engines, machines and buildings.

• Maths is the study of shapes and how numbers work together.

Cool jobs for the future

People doing the cool jobs in this book were once children excited by STEM skills at school. If you are interested in these skills, you might just find a future career for yourself in this book.

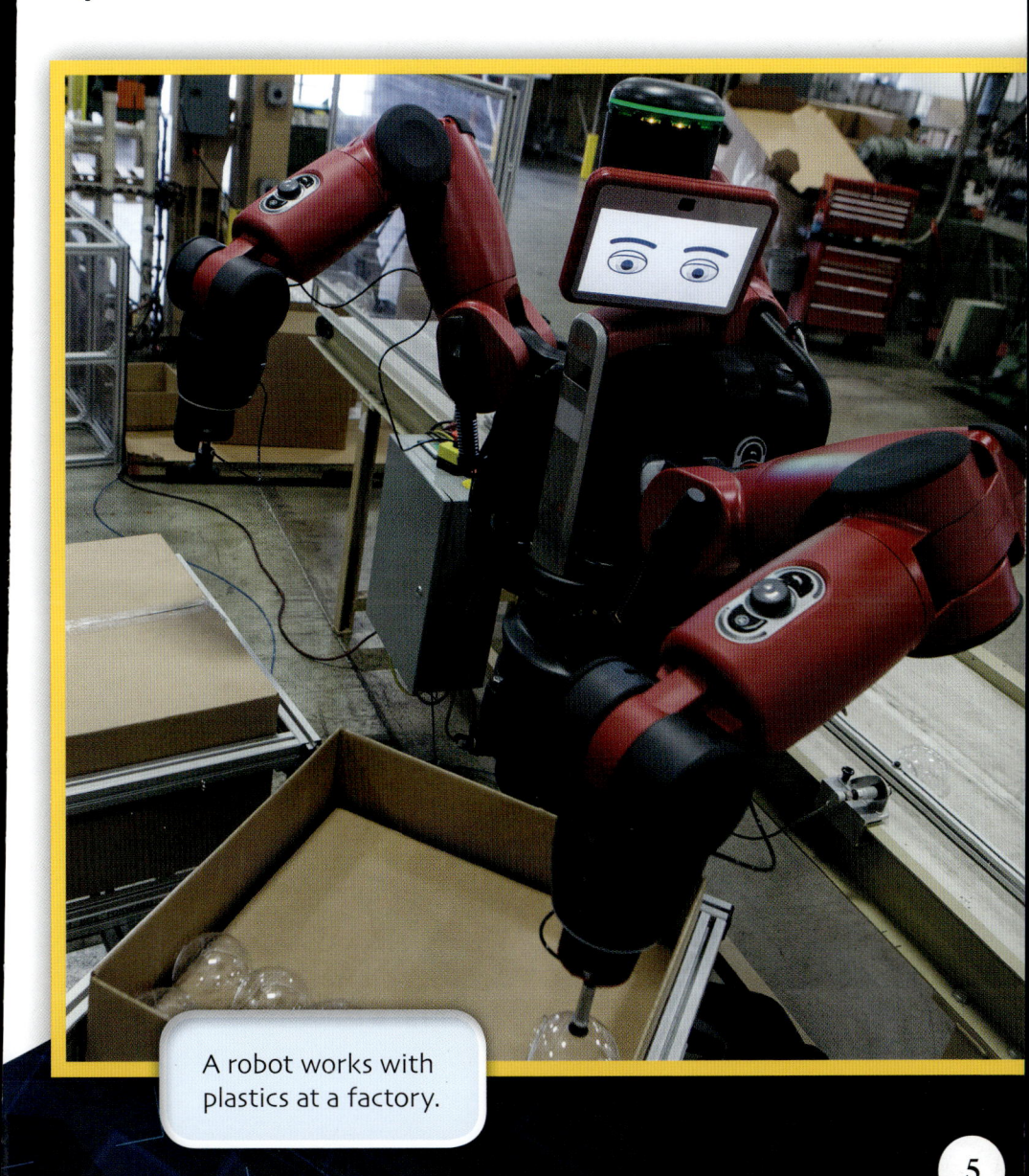

A robot works with plastics at a factory.

Chapter 1
Robotics

Robots are all around us. These machines are able to do jobs by themselves. A computer often controls them. Some, such as toy robots, entertain us. But others work for us, such as robot vacuum cleaners. Robots make vehicles in factories, help unwell people in hospitals, go on military missions and do many other useful jobs.

Different types of robots

Robots are created to do certain jobs. Robots that crush rocks work in the coal mining business. Soldiers use robots to take apart bombs a safe distance away from people. Many robots are powerful robotic arms that can grip, lift, spray and do many other tasks in factories.

In demand

Robots are in great demand in many types of businesses. They can be programmed to do the same task time after time without getting tired or making mistakes. Fires, explosions and falls can injure people. Using robots instead can decrease these risks. With a *remote control*, people can run robots while staying away from dangerous areas.

Robots weld to form car bodies in this car factory.

Roboticist

Would you like to invent a new robot dinosaur for a theme park or a life-size robot that could play hockey? Roboticists invent, design and build some amazing robots.

Designed with purpose

A roboticist designs robots for specific jobs. Some robots need wheels to move around, but others have bodies that fit into narrow spaces. Some have long arms with tools at the end to work on machines. Many robots need to have built-in *sensors*. For example, some robots are designed to find sources of pollution. They have sensors that can find harmful materials such as lead or other metals.

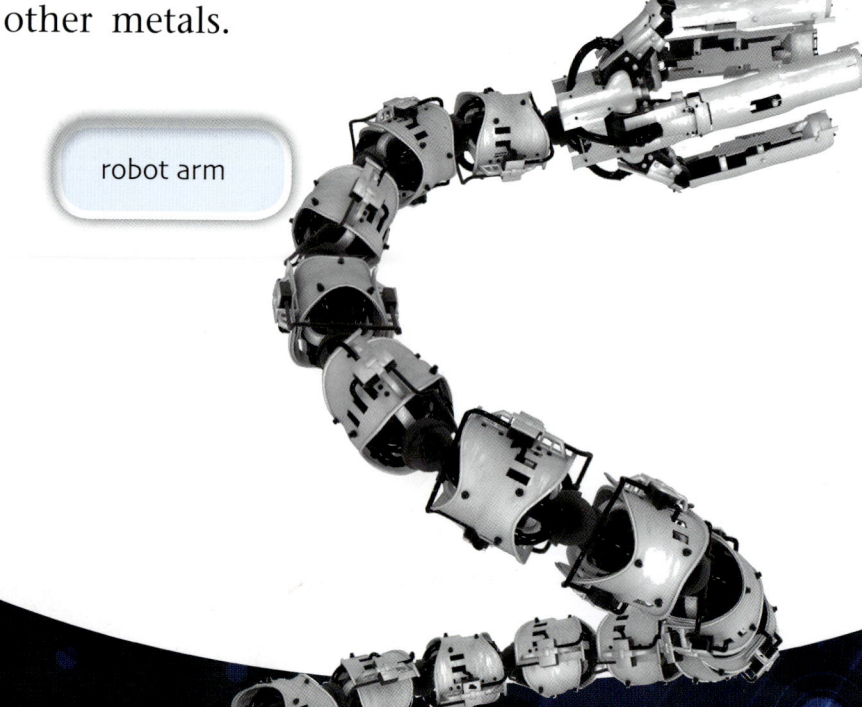

robot arm

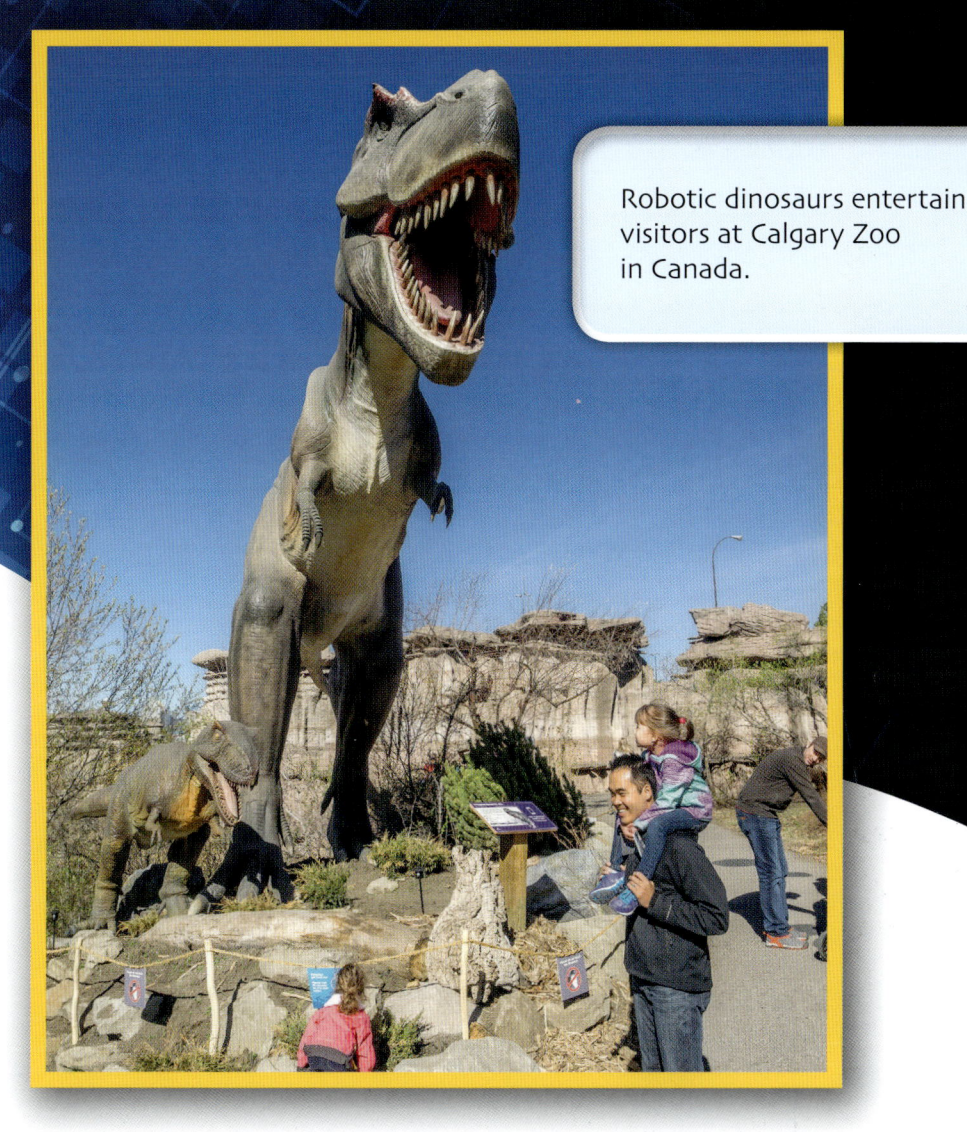

Robotic dinosaurs entertain visitors at Calgary Zoo in Canada.

Robot controls and testing

Roboticists also need to make the equipment that controls robots, such as computers. These computers are often very small.

After robots are put together, roboticists test their robots to make sure they work properly. They may need to make changes.

Drone engineer

Is it a bird? Is it a plane? No, it's a drone! The word "drone" usually means a flying robot. Some are small with many spinning *propellers*, while others are huge with wings.

Help from above

Drones help people in many ways. They can help spot criminals in a crowd of people or film weddings or scenes for films from the air. Air forces use large, fast drones to spy on enemies. Scientists use small drones to study wildlife.

The US RQ-4 Global Hawk military drone has high-quality cameras to spy on enemies.

An octocopter has eight rotors that spin to lift it into the air. These drones can carry heavy cameras.

drone frame

Designing drones

Drone engineers decide what a drone will look like. They build its frame and plan how to power its motors. They design computer programs to control the drone. They need to work out how to communicate with the drone in the air. They may also fit cameras onto the drone. People who fly drones can use them to take videos or photos.

AI engineer

AI stands for *artificial intelligence.* AI engineers make robots that can think like humans!

How it works

People make decisions based on what they have done and learned in the past. AI engineers create robots and other machines that can make decisions based on past actions, too. They may design computer programs that learn what you buy online, so they can make suggestions of what else you might like to buy. The more you shop, the better they will be at guessing what you will like.

Different types of AI

AI engineers create all kinds of robots. They make robots that can play chess. They also make more useful robotic machines. When a hospital scanning machine looks inside a patient's body, AI systems often study the images. They learn to recognize patterns that might be signs of a health problem. AI systems can become faster and better than humans at this job.

A man plays chess with a robot. Many of these robots can learn based on the moves of the person playing against them.

Chapter 2

Computers

It's hard to imagine a world without computers, whether they are notebooks, PCs or tablets. Computers store, find and process information, or *data*. They also send and receive it. But they are pretty useless without the programs, or software, that make them work.

Software developers

Software developers speak a special language: code! They put together sets of instructions written in a computer coding language. The instructions create a program. Some programs are apps that people can use to track their fitness or to play music. Some programs control the amount of energy machines use. These computer programs are meant to help save energy. They can be included on everything from dishwashers to aircraft carriers.

Development process

Software developers may write code from scratch or change coding that is already in use. But their work does not stop there. They also test the software to find and fix any problems.

Software developers write and test code.

Web designer

When you click on a website, have you ever wondered who makes those pages look so colourful and tempting to open? Web designers use their skills to create websites used around the world.

Good websites

Web designers work with customers to decide how a web page will look. A good website is one that works easily and quickly without crashing. It has an eye-catching design, interesting information, clear pictures and well-written text.

Getting it out there

Web designers use code to organize the information. This includes places on pages where users can fill in data, such as addresses. They also put the website onto the internet. They give information about the site to search engines such as Google so people can find it.

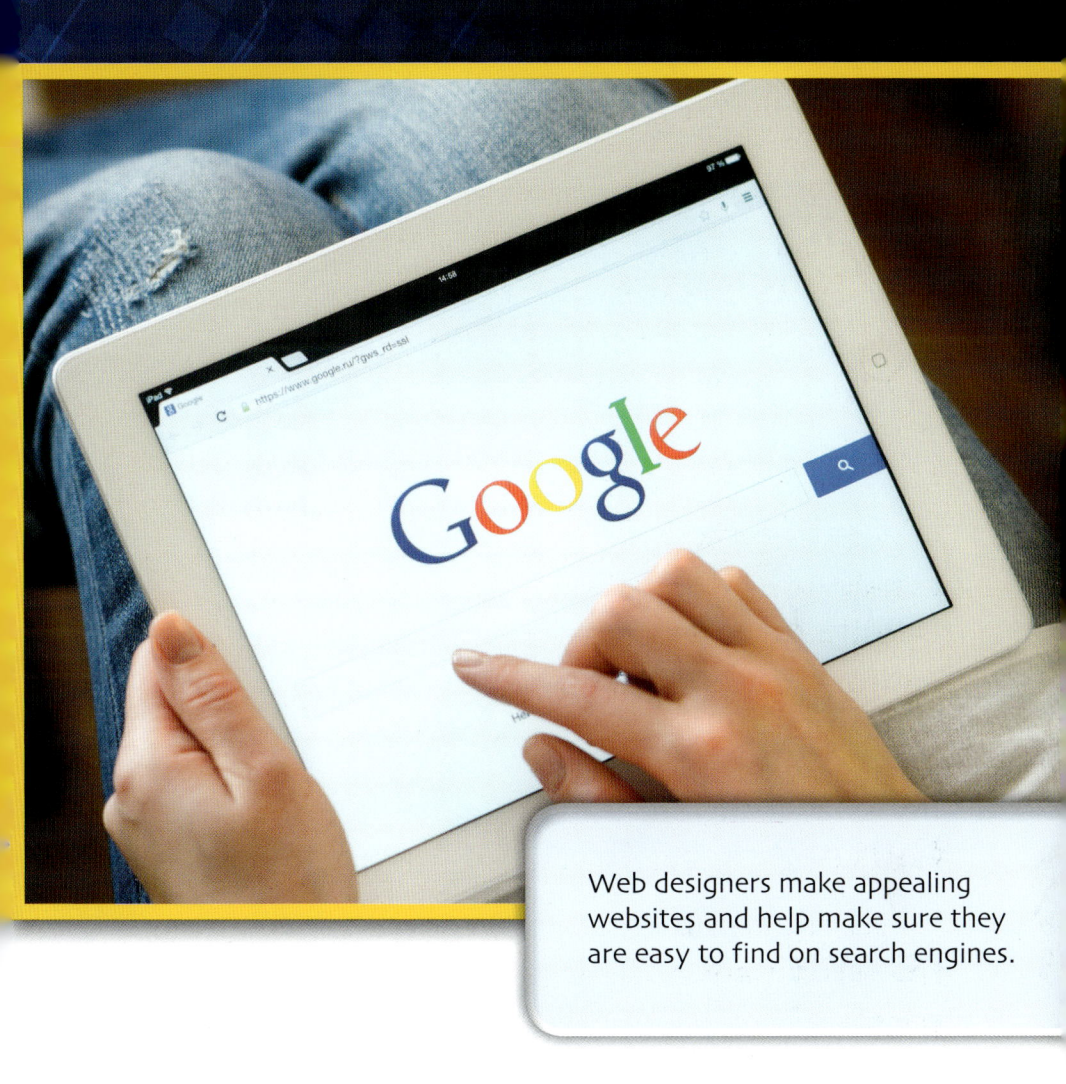

Web designers make appealing websites and help make sure they are easy to find on search engines.

FACT
Every second there are more than 55,000 searches on the Google website.

Internet security analyst

There is a war going on across the internet. Criminals are using websites to steal money or secret information from people. Some studies say cyberattacks cost businesses more than £300 billion every year. But internet security analysts are fighting back!

Internet security analysts have computer systems that help them find signs of criminal activity.

Making websites more secure

Internet security analysts make websites safer for people to use. They monitor, or watch, website use for anything that seems out of the ordinary, such as a great deal of money disappearing from someone's online bank account. Analysts try to stop criminals getting data from computers. They give information they find that could help identify criminals to police. They help improve antivirus software. This software helps protect computers against viruses sent by criminals. These viruses are designed to help people steal information or destroy data on computers.

Staying aware

Internet security analysts are always on the lookout for new internet crimes. They help to work out ways of responding to these threats before too much damage has been done.

Chapter 3
Gaming

Do you love playing video games like Angry Birds, Pokémon GO or Minecraft? Then your dream job could be in the video game industry.

Not just for fun

Many video games are played for fun. Others teach skills. For example, some games help students learn foreign languages. Flight *simulators* use games that help pilots learn to fly while they are safe on the ground. The pilots use controllers similar to those in a plane. The computer program makes it seem like the pilots are in a real plane.

Playing games

Can you imagine being paid to play video games? Games testers spend hours doing just that, but they have a serious job to do. They tell games companies about any problems they find in a game, such as difficulty moving between levels. Some gamers are paid to play video games. They often play in teams in front of hundreds of people. The winners can earn big cash prizes.

Gamers stay focused as they play in a video game tournament in California, USA.

Who buys the most video games?

Do you know a lot of people who play video games? The number of people buying and playing video games depends on where you live. Video game companies make the most earnings from these 10 countries.

Rank	Country	Total games revenues (in millions of pounds)
1	China	19,560.8
2	United States	18,942.4
3	Japan	9,991.7
4	South Korea	3,248.8
5	Germany	3,225.8
6	United Kingdom	3,074.5
7	France	2,197.7
8	Spain	1,454.5
9	Canada	1,438.6
10	Italy	1,398.4

Data from Newzoo 2016 Global Games Market Report (as of June 2016)

Games designer

Have you ever played a video game and thought, *I could do better than that?* Perhaps you could be a game designer, creating whole new worlds for gamers to enjoy.

Many tasks

Some games designers have the ideas for games or write game stories. They decide the basic plot of the game. Others decide the levels and rules of the game. There are also people who do the coding to create characters and settings.

Interested in a gaming job? Here are some tips:

- Try lots of different types of games to learn more about what works and what doesn't.
- Learn some basic coding to make characters move or to make simple games.
- Read books about video game design.
- Take an interest in subjects that you don't normally research. You never know where an idea for a great game might come from!
- Learn about *graphic* design. Practise making posters on a computer. Have fun trying different things with the layout, for example, by moving the type and images.

A games designer works on a game at the Wooga company in Berlin, Germany.

Virtual reality engineer

Have you ever thought about what it might be like to enter a new world? You can find out by stepping into a virtual reality (VR) video game!

A man plays a video game with a virtual reality headset.

Amazing worlds

Virtual reality is an imaginary world created by a computer. The world is *three-dimensional* (3-D). VR engineers design and create these worlds so they look real to gamers. They create special equipment for gamers to wear, such as headsets and goggles. Gloves can allow wearers to feel as if they can touch, move and work with the objects they find inside the VR world.

Beyond games

VR engineers may create worlds to help people. For example, people with a fear of spiders or a fear of heights can use VR headsets to face their fears in a realistic digital world. This is far less stressful than facing the real thing.

Chapter 4
Product design

What makes people pick a certain pair of trainers or choose one jacket instead of another? There are secrets to knowing how to make things people want to buy!

What people want

The look, feel and ease of use of any product can greatly affect whether people want to buy it or not. There may be thousands of ideas for new products, but only some are successful. This is partly because of the materials chosen, how much they cost to make and what is popular.

High-tech jobs involving products

Many types of high-tech jobs involve products. Some people design products, while others build them. Some people work in factories developing new machines or ways of making products in large quantities for the public to buy. Others use scientific skills to develop new materials, such as waterproof fabrics that let air pass through them.

Apple has built a successful business making computers, mobile phones and other devices. Product designers sometimes get ideas about how to improve products from customers.

Product designer

Take a look around you. No matter which man-made object catches your eye, a product designer invented it.

It all starts with an idea

Product designers start off with an idea for a product. It may be their idea or one that a customer gives them. Then they make sketches of the possible shape, colour and form of the product. Designers choose materials that suit the purpose of the product. They might choose hard metal to make a bicycle frame or heat-proof plastic to make a kettle.

Testing

Product designers find out many things about their products by testing a *prototype*. This model shows what the product will look like. It is better to test a product to see if it works properly and looks right before a company spends time and money making the product in large numbers.

A man works on a prototype for a remote control plane.

Mobile phone designer

Mobile phones need to look great but be tough. They have to be able to do lots of tasks, from taking photos to answering spoken questions. Mobile phone designers have a big job to do.

Many parts

Designers need to make sure all the parts of a mobile phone work well together in a small space. Some of these parts include a camera, a microphone, a rechargeable battery and a computer to run software.

Practical design

Designers make mobile phones that are built for everyday use. They choose tough, lightweight materials such as plastics. They design products that work with today's software yet are ready for future upgrades. The upgrades improve the way the phone works.

Fact

There are more than 4.5 billion mobile phone users worldwide. That's nearly two-thirds of all the people on Earth!

Workers put mobile phones together at a factory in China.

Timeline of mobile phone development

1973   Dr Martin Cooper makes the first call on a mobile phone he invented.
1983   The first mobile phone, the Motorola DynaTAC, goes on sale.
1989   The first flip phone, the Motorola MicroTAC, is released.
1994   The IBM Simon is released. It is the first smartphone with a touch screen.
1999   The first mass-market mobile phone, the Nokia 3210/3310, is released. More than 150 million are sold.
2000   The first camera phone, the J-SH04, is released.
2007   The Apple iPhone becomes the first finger-operated touch screen mobile phone.
2014   The Huawei MediaPad X1 is released. It has the largest screen yet seen on a mobile phone.
2014   The Vivo X5 Max is released. It is the thinnest mobile phone yet made.

3-D printing engineer

From jet parts and jewellery to toys that children design themselves, 3-D printing is changing the world! This amazing new technology prints 3-D objects by adding layer upon layer of materials such as plastic.

Printing with different materials

The people who invent and make these machines are 3-D printing engineers. They test out different materials to print with, such as glass and steel.

These engineers are in demand because printing objects can be faster and cheaper than making them in factories. The objects are exact copies of the ideas that people have designed on computers. 3-D objects that are already being printed include toys, masks, parts for wheelchairs and new designs for buildings.

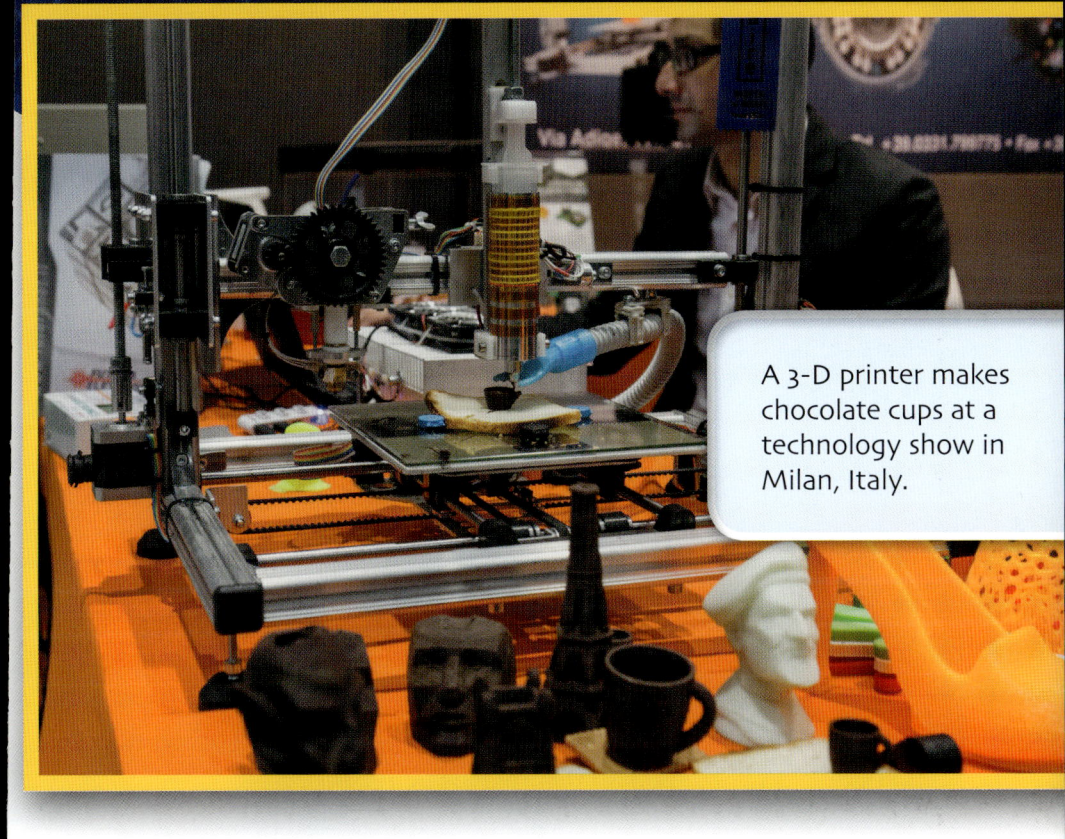

A 3-D printer makes chocolate cups at a technology show in Milan, Italy.

A designer measures a model in a 3-D design studio.

33

Chapter 5
Biomedicine

Biomedicine is a mix of biology and medicine. In biomedicine, people use STEM skills to solve health and other problems in living things.

Biomedicine at work

Some people who work in biomedicine study tiny living things called bacteria that can cause diseases. They try to find ways to stop disease-causing bacteria from spreading. Other workers study how living things handle extreme environments, such as space.

Biomedical engineering

Biomedical engineers invent, design and build things to help people. Some create man-made body parts, or *prostheses*, such as hearts or legs for people who are unwell or who have been injured in accidents.

Fact
The earliest man-made leg dates back to about 2,400 years ago.

Some biomedical engineers develop special robot surgical systems. These systems are very helpful in many hospitals. That's because surgeons can use them to carry out very delicate and detailed operations with less risk to patients.

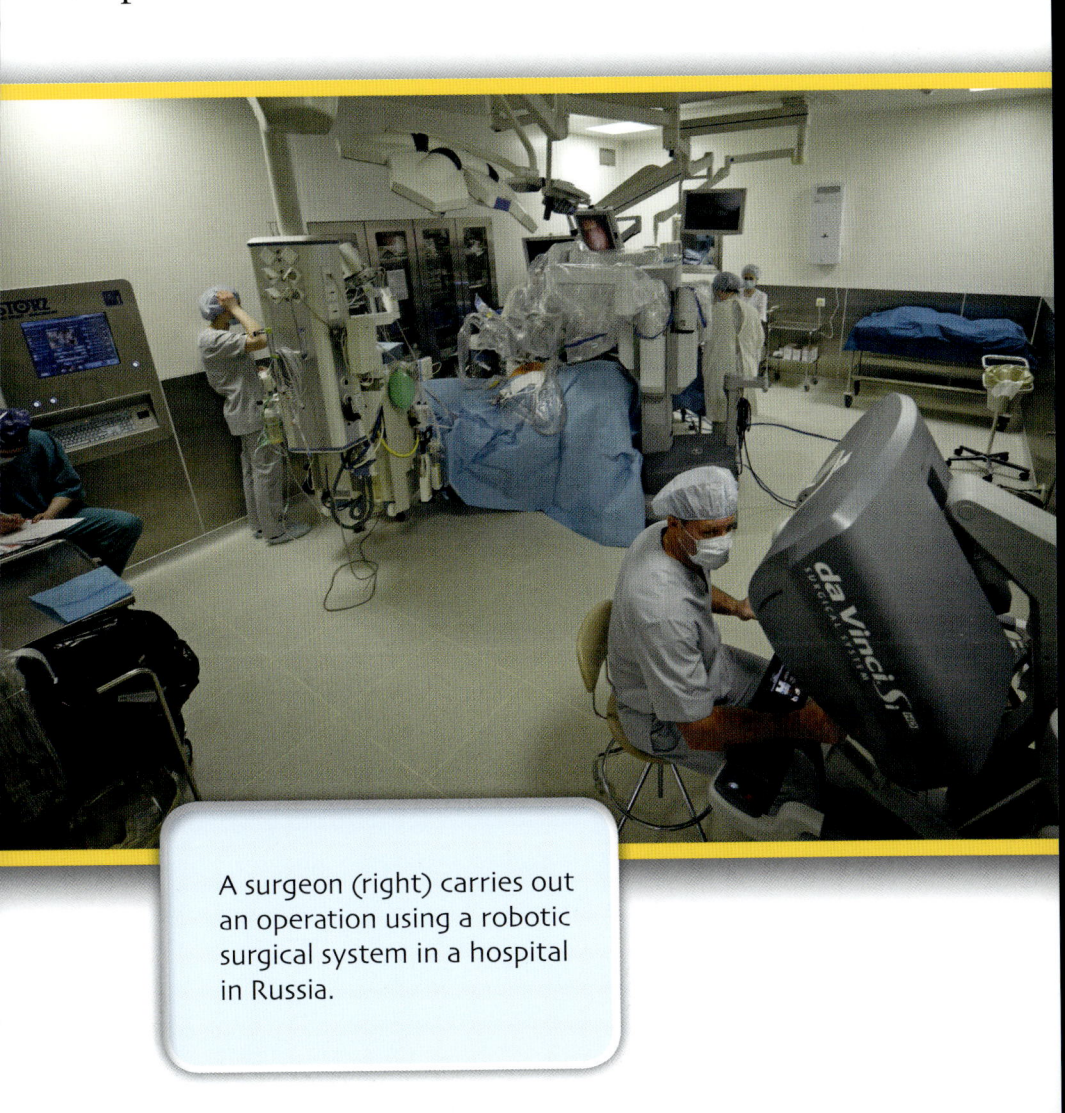

A surgeon (right) carries out an operation using a robotic surgical system in a hospital in Russia.

Animal prosthetics designer

Animal *prosthetics* designers save animals' lives. By fitting a new beak on a bird with a broken one, the bird can eat again. These designers also make prostheses to improve lives for animals.

Helping a variety of animals

Many prosthetics designers work on pets or animals in wildlife parks. They make parts to fit certain animals, such as a new back leg for an old dog or a fin for an injured dolphin. They need to carefully choose materials. For example, a beak needs to be tough but also lightweight, so it does not weigh down the bird's head.

Sometimes designers make parts that do not match the originals. They may attach a set of wheels to the bottom of a tortoise's shell to help a tortoise that has only one leg move around.

A trainer works with a dolphin with a prosthetic tail.

Nanotechnologist

Nanotechnologists are people whose job is to think small! They design and produce objects, machines and other items that can be a thousand times thinner than a sheet of paper!

Small world

Everything in the world is made from tiny building blocks called *atoms*. Nanotechnologists use microscopes to see and to control atoms. They do this to change the features of materials. For example, they might make a material stronger or more waterproof.

Different businesses

Nanotechnologists work in many businesses. Some design smaller, longer-lasting batteries for cars, mobile phones or other machines. Others work in health care. They have found ways to treat cancer using tiny machines that deliver drugs to treat the exact places in the body where cancer is growing. This means the cancer drugs cause less damage to healthy parts of a patient's body.

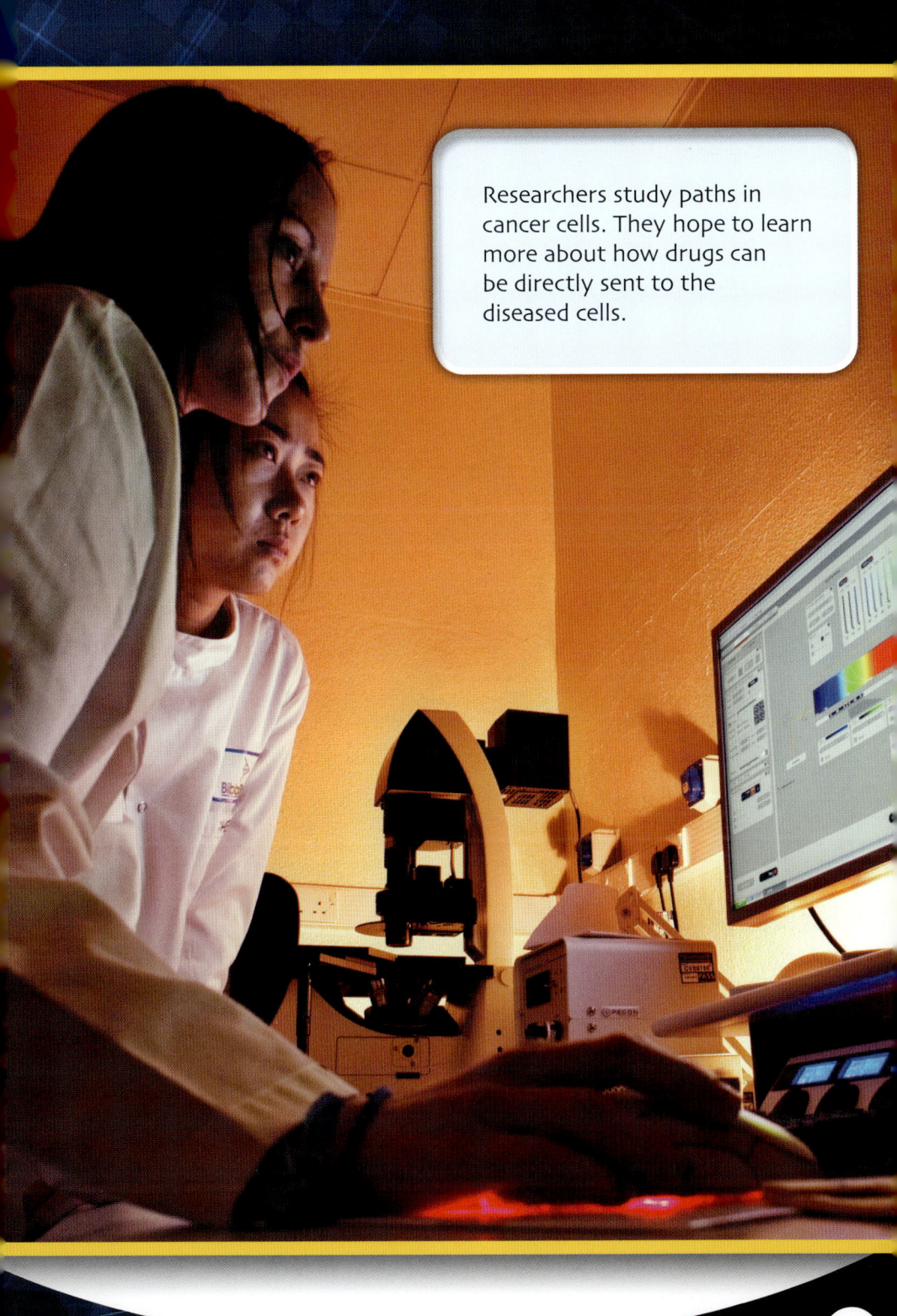

Researchers study paths in cancer cells. They hope to learn more about how drugs can be directly sent to the diseased cells.

Forensic scientist

Crime scene investigators (CSIs) have the gruesome job of searching for clues at crime scenes. They often need the expert help of forensic scientists to further study clues to solve the crimes.

Scientific proof

Forensic scientists study materials left behind at crime scenes. A hair might fall out of a robbery suspect's head at a house that was burgled. Scientists may be able to identify the suspect from the hair. Police can use this as proof that the person was there. Forensic samples can often be used to help prove or disprove ideas presented in a criminal case.

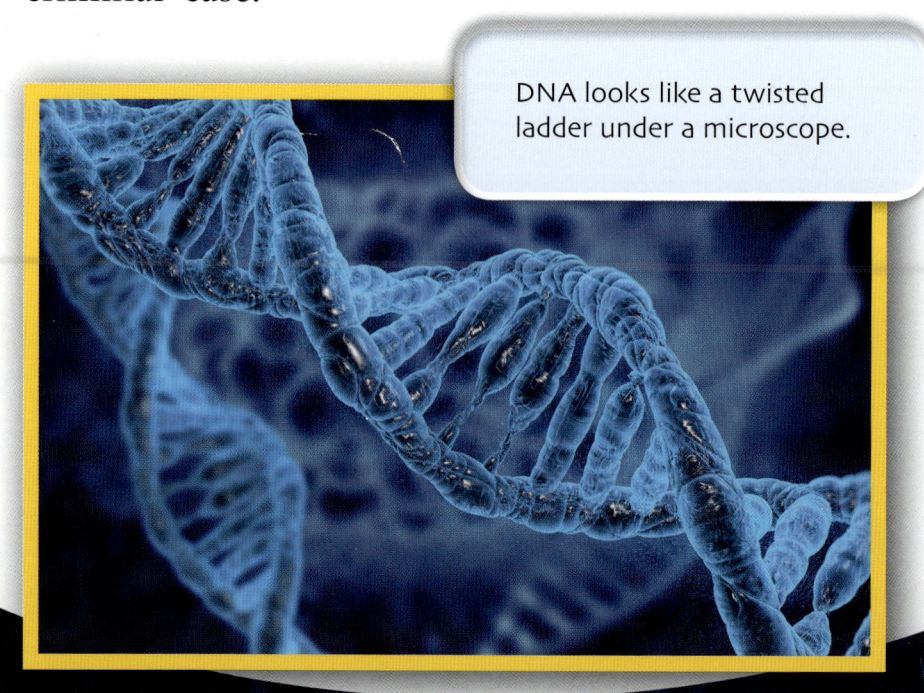

DNA looks like a twisted ladder under a microscope.

Crime scene investigators use many tools at a crime scene to look for clues.

Special skills

Forensic scientists have special skills. Some work in labs doing tests on crime scene samples, such as hair, saliva or blood. *DNA* tests can tell who the samples came from using information stored inside cells. Other scientists study bullets to identify which guns fired them.

Entomologist

Can you imagine working with creepy crawlies? Entomologists are scientists who study insects. Many of them help to limit the insects' harmful effects on people.

Types of entomologist

Entomologists often focus their work in a certain area. Some study how to stop pests from eating crops or harming forests. They also find ways to make the numbers of helpful insects, such as bees and ladybirds, grow. Bees help crops by pollinating flowers as they move between plants searching for food. Without bees, we could not grow as much food. Ladybirds eat thousands of pests that destroy crops. Other entomologists research ways to stop insects from spreading diseases that affect millions of people every year.

Pollen from flowers sticks to a bee's body. When the bee moves to another plant, the pollen is carried onto the plant. Many crops need this pollination to produce fruit or seeds.

An entomologist groups dead insects at a park in Costa Rica. Collections like these can help track changes in insect populations over time. The insects have been treated with chemicals to stop their bodies breaking down.

43

Biotechnologist

Biotechnologists use their knowledge of living things to help feed, clean and even heal the world.

Helping crops grow

Some biotechnologists help farmers grow more food. They develop crops that grow bigger, more quickly or with more flavour. Some grow plants that can fight off disease or survive lack of water caused by drought. They also invent and grow new foods in labs, such as a meat-like product called Quorn.

Problem-solving

Other biotechnologists focus on problem-solving. They make systems to clean water so it is safe to use and drink. In some places they have used certain types of bacteria to clean oil spills from the sea. Some invent ways of making new types of fuel that can power our machines without producing smoke and fumes that harm Earth's atmosphere.

Biotechnologists may need to test samples in labs.

Scientists gather samples from polluted water.

45

Chapter 6
Earth science

Earth is an amazing lump of rock floating in space. Some people have the job of studying what Earth is made from and how it works.

Types of Earth scientist

Some Earth scientists study what our planet is like deep inside. Others find natural resources such as oil and metals from underground rocks. These metals include steel and gold.

Volcanologist

Volcanologists study volcanoes. They are the most daring of Earth scientists. When volcanoes erupt, gases and hot, melted rock called magma burst out of Earth's surface. These bursts can injure and kill people living nearby. Volcanologists try to find out when they are going to erupt, so they can warn people.

Fact
Researchers estimate that more than 500 volcanoes are active around the world.

Volcanologists take a lava sample in Hawaii. Their suits help protect them from the heat.

Interview

Rebecca Coats, volcanologist

What do you do in your job?

I mainly work in my lab. I conduct lots of experiments, from pressing and heating rocks to breaking magmas. This shows me how strong rocks are and how they might behave in an eruption or in other conditions. On other days I visit volcanoes to take measurements and rock samples from volcanoes.

Which skills are most useful in your job?

Maths and English are both very useful. With good maths and English skills, much of science can be learned later on. We use maths to calculate what might happen at volcano sights and English to tell people about it.

Why do you think volcanology is important?

Many people live around active volcanoes because the soil around these areas is very rich. By watching volcanoes closely and using data from experiments, we can get a good idea about when they will erupt and how forcefully. This can help save people's lives.

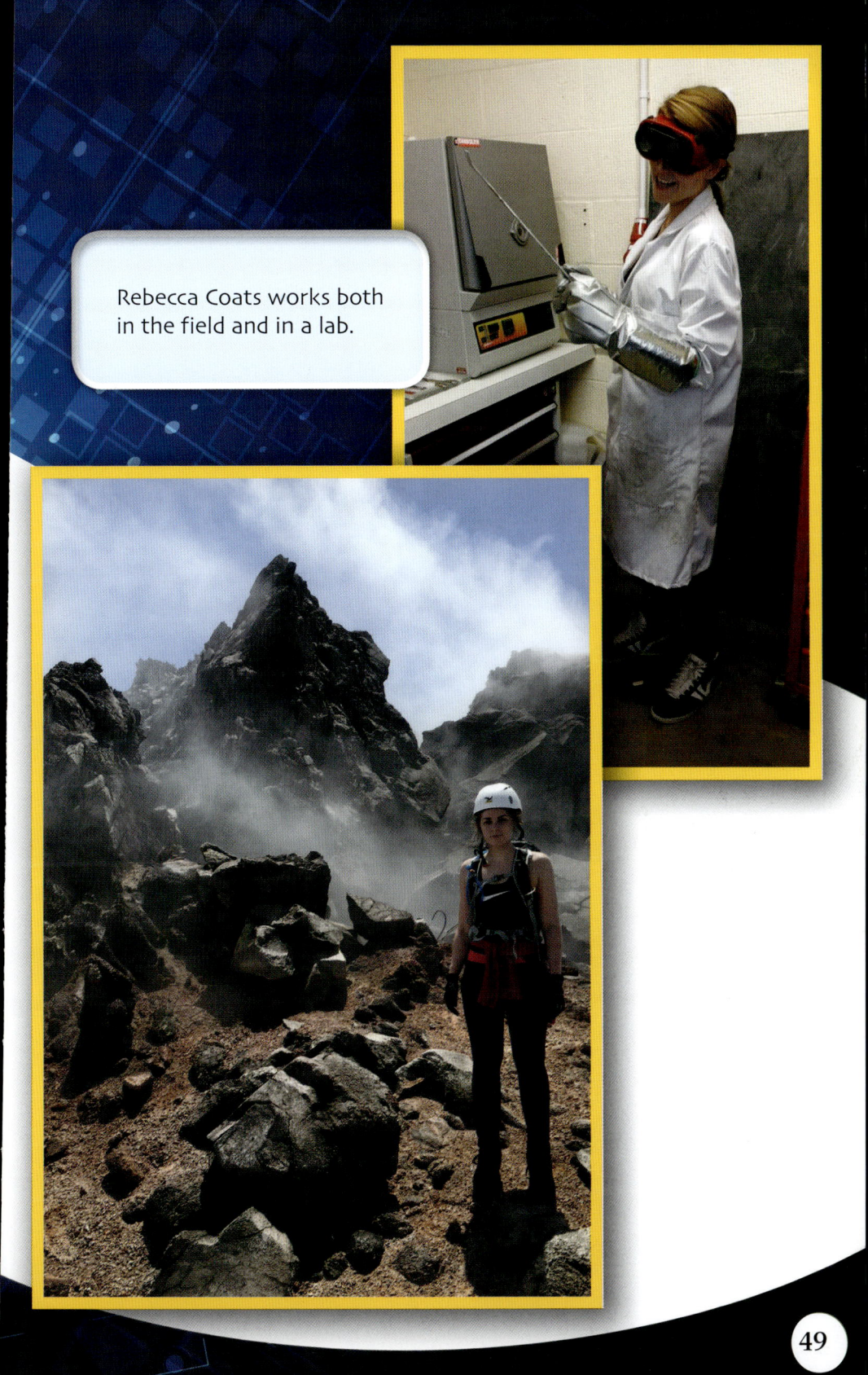

Rebecca Coats works both in the field and in a lab.

Storm chasers

Most people race to get out of the way when there's a hurricane or tornado coming. Storm chasers do the opposite. They get up close to these dangerous storms to study them!

Study of weather

Some people chase storms as a hobby. They like to watch or record extreme weather. Others are meteorologists. These scientists use a variety of tools to study and record weather. They use foam pads that show the size of hailstones that fall into them. They use radar systems. Radar sends out radio waves. When the waves hit something such as rain or snow, they bounce back. Scientists can then tell where the rain or snow is falling. Radar can also measure wind speed close to the ground.

Into the storm

Meteorologists follow tornadoes in vehicles and fly close to or even into hurricanes in aircraft. They use sensors to measure wind speed and direction and air temperature. Some sensors are inside metal tubes that planes drop into hurricanes. These sensors fall to Earth, sending information about storms to computers.

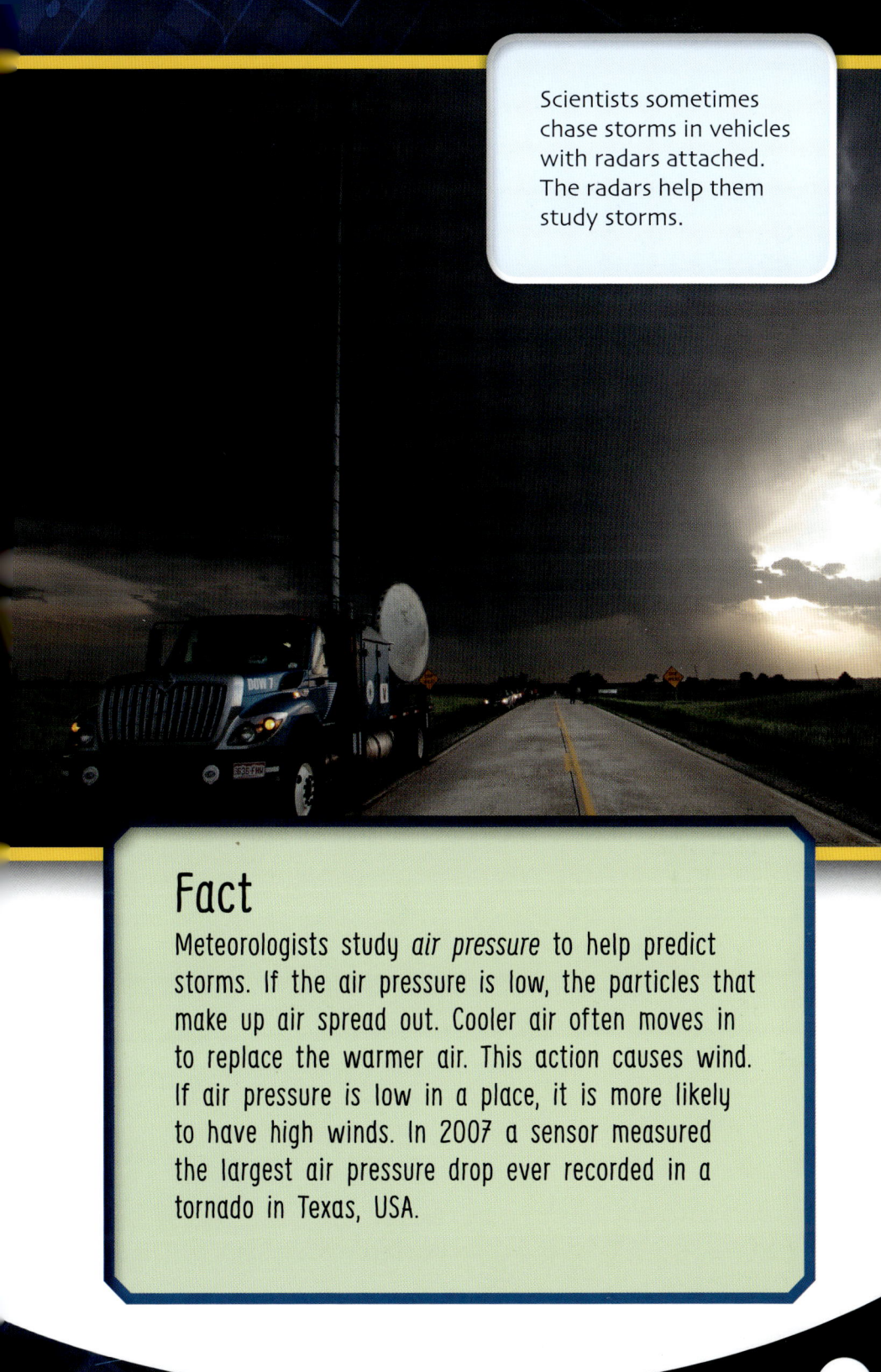

Scientists sometimes chase storms in vehicles with radars attached. The radars help them study storms.

Fact

Meteorologists study *air pressure* to help predict storms. If the air pressure is low, the particles that make up air spread out. Cooler air often moves in to replace the warmer air. This action causes wind. If air pressure is low in a place, it is more likely to have high winds. In 2007 a sensor measured the largest air pressure drop ever recorded in a tornado in Texas, USA.

Chapter 7
Transport and energy

Imagine how amazing it would be to find new ways to transport people around the planet or to make energy to power the world's machines.

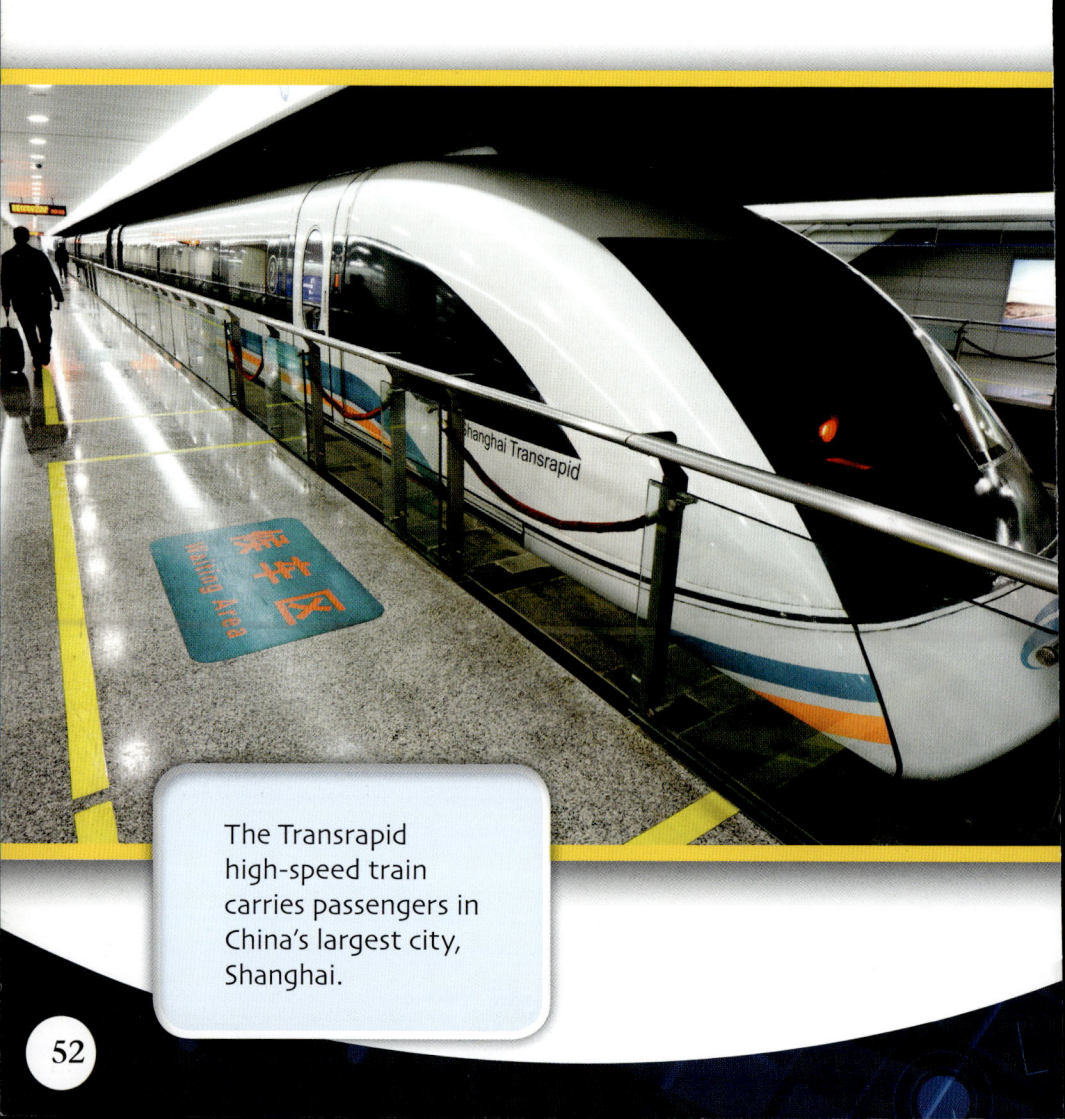

The Transrapid high-speed train carries passengers in China's largest city, Shanghai.

Fact

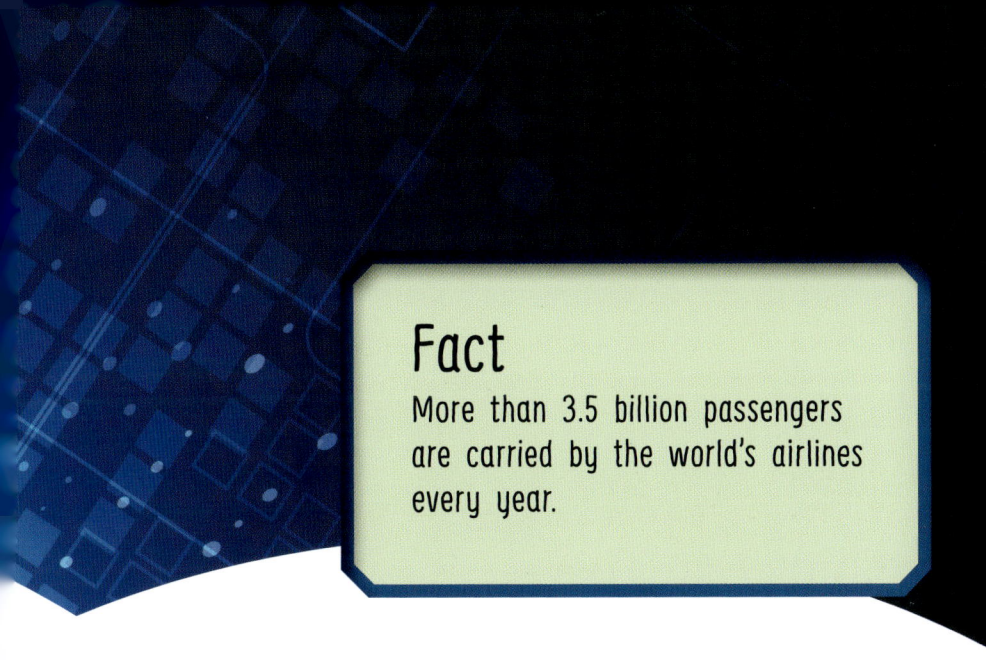

More than 3.5 billion passengers are carried by the world's airlines every year.

Getting around

Many jobs help get people and goods from place to place. Transport engineers create motorways, airports and railways. Marine engineers design, build and test ocean vehicles. These include submarines as well as very large cargo ships that carry goods.

Urban transportation

Much of the world's population lives in crowded cities. Transportation planners design ways to move people safely and quickly around busy cities. They work to develop systems of underground tunnels and electric trains.

Aircraft engineer

The sky's the limit for some people's jobs. Aircraft engineers create and design amazing vehicles that move through the air. These include military fighter planes, helicopters and giant jets that carry hundreds of people.

Designed to fly

Aircraft engineers develop light, strong materials to build aircraft that can withstand great speeds. They design shapes of wings and propellers that allow aircraft to take off, stay in the air and land, time after time. Aircraft engineers invent equipment too. Pilots may use it to fly the aircraft.

Testing

Aircraft engineers work out how an aircraft should perform and test it carefully before it takes flight. They test the aircraft's engines, landing gear and brakes. They also test the comfort and safety of passenger seats.

An engineer checks the engine of a passenger plane.

55

Rocket scientist

Rocket scientists design and test rockets that carry spacecraft beyond Earth. These rockets fly faster than the speed of sound!

Rocket power

Rocket scientists invent and test powerful engines to carry heavy rockets into space. These engines move the rockets forwards by pushing hot gases out backwards. They also make systems to steer and guide rockets. These systems must stay in contact with the rockets from great distances.

What's on rockets

Some rockets carry items to space. They carry *satellites* that help us communicate with one another around the globe. They also carry equipment needed in space stations where astronauts live in space. For example, some spacecraft bring necessary items to the International Space Station (ISS).

Fact
Rockets travel faster than 7.8 kilometres per second to reach space.

Engineers prepare to join a space capsule with a rocket engine.

The robotic arm of the ISS (right) grabs the HTV-6 cargo vehicle. The vehicle delivers supplies to the ISS.

57

Energy engineer

Have you ever switched on a light, and nothing happened? The power was out! Our world would be very different without power. We have energy engineers to thank for designing and building the machines to produce the power we need.

Using many energy sources

Some engineers work with non-renewable energy sources such as coal. Others work with renewable energy, which comes from a natural source that cannot run out. For example, some work with solar energy. They use equipment that captures energy from the sun to make electricity. Engineers may also create wind or water *turbines*. These machines turn wind or moving water energy into electricity.

Power plants

Energy engineers also plan the building of power plants where electricity is made. They decide where to put them. For example, wind farms need to be in places with strong winds.

Engineers review plans for a solar rooftop.

Future jobs

Can you imagine your amazing future career yet? Just think, you could do any of these jobs and many more with great STEM skills.

Skills in demand

STEM skills are in demand! In many places, the number of STEM job openings is growing faster than the number of openings for other types of jobs. Wages for STEM jobs are often higher than they are for non-STEM jobs, too.

You can learn more about science, technology, engineering and maths by participating in competitions.

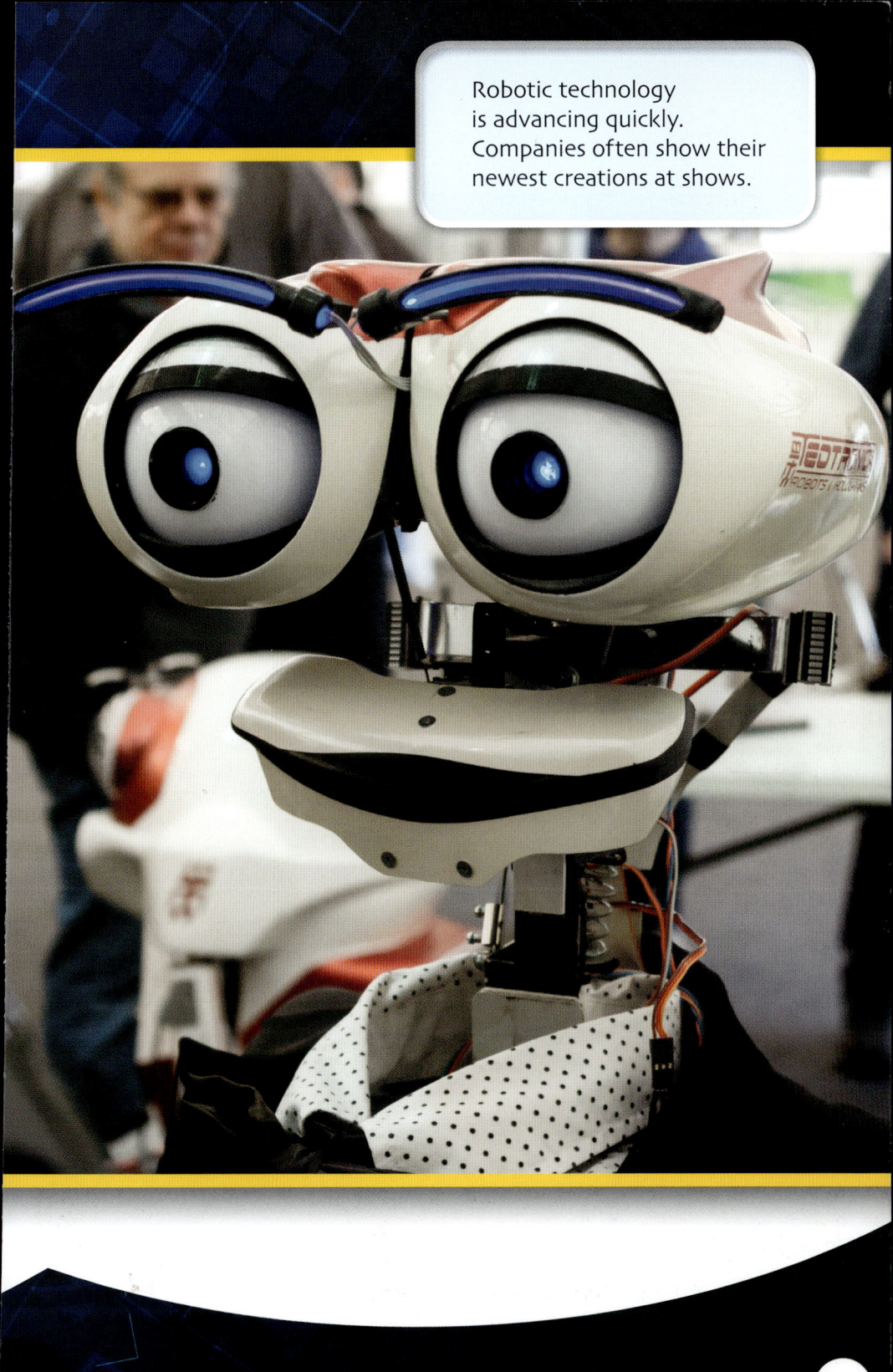

Robotic technology is advancing quickly. Companies often show their newest creations at shows.

Changes to come

Not long ago, there were no drones or self-driving vehicles, yet today people have jobs creating them. There will be more cool jobs in the future as technology changes. There may even be completely new jobs no one has thought of yet! What will you do?

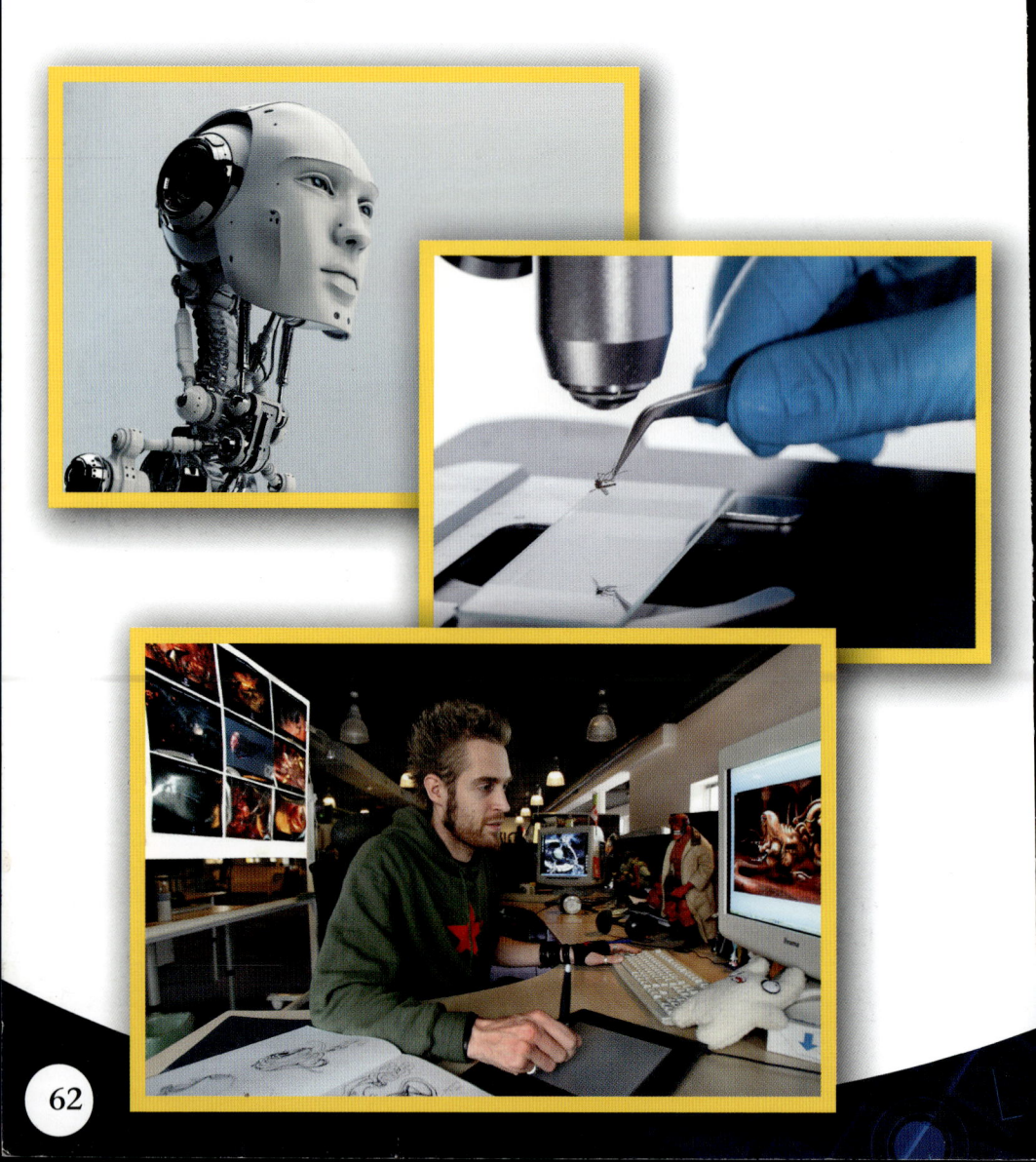

Glossary

air pressure force of air pushing against something

artificial intelligence developing computer systems that can learn and make decisions

atom element in its smallest form

data information such as numbers and characters usually stored or processed on computers

DNA material in cells that gives people their individual characteristics; DNA stands for deoxyribonucleic acid

engineering work of designing structures, products and systems

graphic visual image such as an illustration, photograph or work of art

propeller rotating blade that moves a vehicle through air or water

prosthesis man-made limb or body part

prosthetic relating to a prosthesis

prototype early version of an object, device or machine to test how it works or its qualities

remote control device used to control machines from a distance

satellite spacecraft that circles Earth; satellites gather and send information

sensor device that detects change, such as heat, light, sound and motion

simulator device that reproduces what actually occurs in reality

technology use of science to do practical things, such as designing complex machines

three-dimensional having or appearing to have length, distance and height; three-dimensional is often shortened to 3-D

turbine machine with blades like a fan that spins with the push of gas or liquid from one direction; the spinning motion is then used to make electricity

Index

3-D printing engineers   32

AI engineers   12
aircraft engineers   54
air pressure   51
animal prosthetics designers   36
artificial intelligence   12

bacteria   34, 44
biomedical engineers   34–35
biotechnologists   44

cameras   11, 30
code   14–15, 16
computer programs   11, 12, 14, 20
cyberattacks   18

DNA   41
drone engineers   10–11
drones   10–11, 62

energy engineers   58
entomologists   42

forensic scientists   40–41

Internet security analysts   18–19

meteorologists   50, 51
mobile phone designers   30
mobile phones   30, 31, 38

nanotechnologists   38

prostheses   34, 36
prototypes   28

remote control   6
roboticists   8–9
robots   6, 8–9, 12, 35
rockets   4, 56
rocket scientists   56

software. *See* computer programs
software developers   14–15
storm chasers   50
surgical systems   35

technology   4, 32, 62
transport engineers   53

video games   20–21, 22
virtual reality engineers   24–25
volcanologists   46, 48

web designers   16
websites   16, 17, 18, 19